DARL – AI Online

Build a Fuzzy Logic Expert System

Andrew N. Edmonds PhD

http://www.docandys.com

Deliberately left blank

Contents

Table of figures.

8

Introduction

Artificial Intelligence is back. It never really went away, but the focus of interest shifted elsewhere over the years. 20 years ago (I was there!) AI was impeded in take up by the slowness of technology, the small size of memory, the difficulty of connecting multiple processors. Most of the learning and inference algorithms now available were in place, but using them was prohibitively expensive for non-trivial problems. Now with the advent of cloud computing and the ease of use and low entry price that cloud computing has bought it's possible for anybody to market an app or web service that uses Artificial intelligence in some form. The only thing missing is the set of tools to implement such a system. This is the reason for DARL.

AI in general – a history

AI has from its inception had two threads: AI inspired by biology, and AI inspired by language and reason.

The purpose of AI has always been to simulate, in some form or other, human intelligence, knowledge and perception. This simulation has focussed on two primary areas (mostly because they were the most accessible): learning relationships from raw data, and encapsulating and reusing knowledge that humans had already acquired.

The first biologically inspired AI system was the Perceptron, introduced in 1957 by Frank Rosenblatt, that intended to copy the behaviour, as it was then understood, of individual brain cells, known as Neurons.

At the same time others, notably Marvin Minsky, were working on the first systems encapsulating human knowledge as rules. The first stage in the battle between biologically inspired AI and rule based AI occurred when Minsky and Pappert wrote a paper pointing out that there was a simple class of relationships that a Perceptron could not learn.

In the hard sciences, people generally frown on solutions that are not complete in some way. In the soft sciences people will grab hold of theories that cover any reasonable sub-set of the data, but that's another story. In any event this was a blow to biologically inspired AI, and one that it did not recover from until the 80s.

Rule based systems were therefore then in the ascendant for many years. In 1986 Rumelhart and McClelland published their book "Parallel Distributed Programming" which demonstrated neural networks that could learn the class of problems the perceptron couldn't, and that could learn any arbitrary function that didn't disappear off to infinity at some point.

By this time, software products began to appear that encapsulated these new ideas. Your humble author wrote the first such commercial software program in Europe, called "Neurun" in 1987.

We now had commercial systems that could learn, though sometimes taking days to process on the existing hardware, and systems that could store human knowledge as rules based on Minsky's work.

It was more a matter of marketing than anything else that separated these two kinds of systems. By the 90s your humble author had created software that could learn rules directly from data, both by a process of fuzzy logic rule induction for examples where example data for the inputs to a problem and the expected outputs were available (supervised learning) and where only input data was available, but some measure of the performance of the created model could be generated (Reinforcement learning). The latter system used Genetic Programming, a form of simulated evolution, to create solutions for otherwise intractable problems, and again your humble author wrote the first papers and designed the first commercial product that combined GP and fuzzy rules.

These products were successful, but were swallowed into the privacy-conscious world of financial trading and were used exclusively by a large futures trading organization. As a result, the arbitrary separation in the collective minds of the marketplace of systems that could learn and systems that could encapsulate human knowledge remained.

In between the 90s and the present this was the pattern. AI was used often for specialized tasks, but built into larger applications, such as Optical Character Recognition, Insurance underwriting or credit scoring.

Things have turned again in the last couple of years. Neural networks have been reborn as Deep Learning, which represents a triumph of truly long term slogging by its inventors, who were present in the last surge in the 80s.

Deep learning has put AI back on the map, and caused others, like Elon Musk, to speculate that AI will surpass, and thus be a menace to, humans in the near future. For the record I don't agree. Deep learning gives us more clues as to how to build human intelligence, but the unifying principle, the thing that makes us grow from a single cell to an intelligent adult is not yet explained, and the solution must lie somewhere in the science of complexity, in self organising systems.

They say a rising tide floats all ships. In this spirit I have dusted off some technology and created lots of new stuff to reoffer my rule based systems software in the DARL suite.

This offers both the ability to take human experience and turn it into rules, and to learn such experience directly from data. The supervised learning system is available now, the reinforcement learning system will be available in SaaS form later.

All this is supplied as a combination of a website offering editing and management, and a web service with a set of REST interfaces. There is also an ever growing set of free example code and free downloadable apps that make it easy for you to build the rule sets you develop into a variety of products created with different technologies and using different media.

Expert systems and DARL

The original formulation of expert systems based on Minsky's work saw knowledge as a "soup" of facts and rules.

The facts were pairs of data items and their values. The rules operated on facts, and allowed you to infer new facts from the current set.

The current state of the expert system was the set of facts and rules in the soup. If you changed anything, like a fact taking on a new value, then potentially everything could change

Conventional expert systems use the Rete algorithm like a net to scoop up from the soup any rules that rely on the changed data item. These rules are then fired, and any data items that are changed are added back to the soup. Again the net is used to search for rules using these new data items, and the process is continued until no data items change.

This means that the amount of time taken to process any change in the data is a-priori indeterminate. Some changes will result in no updates, and others will carry on for many cycles.

Darl has a different architecture. A Darl rule set has a set of inputs and outputs that are defined at the same time as the rules. It's quite permissible to use the outputs of some rules as the inputs for others. This could produce the multi-cycle behaviour of a conventional expert system, instead the rule editing process builds a dependency graph, checks for loops that will cycle forever and creates an execution order that will ensure proper execution in a single pass.

The processing time of Darl is thus predictable and very fast.

Expert systems are well established in areas where the underlying rules do not change. A classic example of this is mathematics, where expert systems are used in software that performs algebraic manipulation and problem solving. In areas where the rules change frequently or are ill defined conventional expert systems have not been so popular.

The reason for this is the complexity of creating and maintaining the rule sets. Firstly, so called "knowledge engineers" are required to create the rule sets and to maintain them, and then there is a subtler problem associated with Boolean logic and real world problems.

In the process of creating and then refining a rule set the knowledge engineers using a Boolean, so conventional, logical system are forced to add more and more rules, or detail to existing rules.

Boolean systems thus can grow very large and thus expensive to maintain. If one were to try, for instance, to model a set of laws, every time a legislation changed, which in some cases is monthly, you would need potentially months of work to ensure your model matched the law.

Darl has several methods for avoiding and neutralising these problems.

The first is what the founder of Fuzzy Logic, Lotfi Zadeh, calls the effect of granular computing. Fuzzy rules are very much more expressive than Boolean rules. Typically, far fewer rules are required for the same problem. Fine tuning is mostly achieved by tinkering with fuzzy set boundaries, which does not result in larger rule sets.

DARL, as you will see, is designed to be very easy to understand and learn to use and "knowledge engineers" are not needed.

Rule sets are modular in Darl. You can treat a rule set as a functional block, like an integrated circuit in electronics, that you wire up to other functional blocks. Thus you can isolate changes to individual blocks, which are individually testable.

Perhaps most importantly, you can create a rule set directly from data using machine learning. These data derived rule sets are identical in structure to the others, although annotated with statistics from the learning process. You can freely mix trained and hand written blocks, and retrain a block in situ.

Fuzzy Logic and Fuzzy Sets

In classical, Boolean logic one can reason with sets, where set membership is clearly defined. For instance, you are either a member of your local gym, or you are not. One can also reason with numeric variables by using bounds, such as > x, < y, etc.

In Fuzzy logic parlance, such sets and limits are called "crisp". This means that membership is sharply defined.

Around 500BC, the Greek philosopher Zeno described a paradox, known as the Sorites Paradox, that illustrates the problem with crisp sets:

- A pile of 2 or 3 stones is a small pile of stones
- If you add a stone to a small pile of stones, it is still a small pile of stones
- Therefore, all piles of stones are small.

There are several conclusions we can draw from this paradox.

Qualitative words like "small" "medium", "large", "high", "low", etc. don't map well onto crisp sets.

It seems that it can be possible to both partly in and partly out of a set.

As more stones are added, the statement "this is a small pile of stones" becomes less true, so truth can be partial.

You can only show that the third line is untrue, and so break the paradox, if you accept that the truth of the statement "this is a small pile of stones" decreases with more stones added; so you must accept that truth can be somewhere between absolute truth and absolute falsehood.

Fuzzy logic is a system of logic that represents truth as a real number between 0 and 1 inclusive. 0 represents absolute falsehood, 1, absolute truth.

The degree of truth of a statement may be anywhere between 0 and 1.

This requires a redefinition of the idea of a set. Fuzzy sets are defined as sets that can an object or state can be a partial member of, i.e. a statement referring to set membership may have partial truth.

The principal use of this idea is for numeric variables, like the number of stones in a pile.

The standard way of representing fuzzy sets is as a chart with the Y axis representing the degree of truth, so 0-1, and the X axis representing the domain of the variable.

So, for instance, if we were to try to describe European male height we might create the following sets:

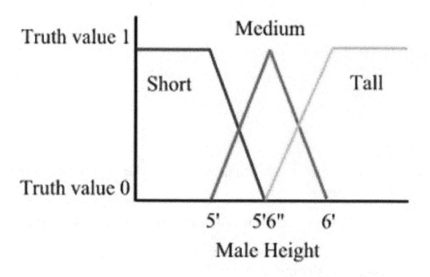

Figure 1, Fuzzy sets for male height

There is no reason why a variety of shapes might not be used for fuzzy sets; the only requirement is that they are convex. However, we have chosen for Darl a simple set of definitions that are very easy to describe.

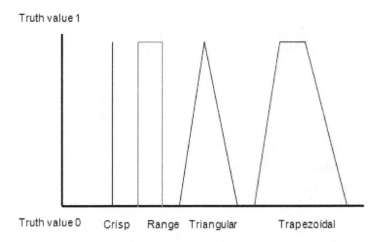

Figure 2, Fuzzy set types

These sets can be described just using an ascending-ordered sequence of numbers representing the intercepts of a vertical line dropped from the vertices to the X axis.

so, the sequence 1,2, represents a range between 1 and 2 inclusive, 1,2,3 represents a triangular fuzzy set peaking at 2, and 4,5,6,7 describes a trapezoid fuzzy set.

Unbounded sets

Some set definitions are unbounded on the left or right. In the case of male height above, the outer sets are unbounded. This is achieved with Darl by using the two keywords *-Infinity*, and *Infinity*. So, using decimal feet rather than feet and inches, the definition of *Short* would be -

`Infinity, 5, 5.5`.

Uncertainty

Uncertainty is the dominant problem in Artificial Intelligence.

Computer programming is mostly about certainty. The operation of a program is hopefully deterministic and certain, the algorithms used have guaranteed characteristics, data items are exact. Behind the scenes, on disk drives and in memory, error correcting algorithms are used to ensure that no cosmic particle or RF burst ever changes data.

As object oriented programming makes explicit, much of programming is about modelling the real world. This could be the state of your bank account, the structure of your company, or any of a million things.

Since the time of Plato, our modelling of the real world has proceeded by assuming perfection: perfect circles, straight lines; and our solving of problems has proceeded by human analysis and algorithm generation.

The world, of course, is not perfect. For many models these imperfections can be ignored, for other models, where mathematical chaos is present for instance, these errors gang up to grow exponentially undermining the viability of any predictions. A classic case of this is Climate Change.

Also, as Gödel showed, many problems are not susceptible to analysis, in that one cannot write an algorithm that will solve all of the variants of the problem all of the time. Inevitably it's the most interesting problems that have this quality.

AI is most useful and most likely to be used where uncertainty is large and where an analytic solution is not available.

Possibility and Probability

Most secondary school and university mathematics courses consider only one form of uncertainty, probability. Measurement uncertainties, in fact all uncertainties are modelled as random processes.

A large algebra has built up around probability. Unfortunately, probability is often mathematically intractable. If you wish to model, for instance, the relationships between disease symptoms and diseases, to perform a kind of supervised learning, using the probabilistic tool of choice, Bayesian belief networks, where disease symptoms and diseases are very large sets, you run into Gödel type problems. Solving any large Bayesian belief network is NP complete, i.e. not guaranteed to be calculable in finite time. Generally, this task can only be performed by breaking the problem down, by saying that some subset symptoms can only possibly be related to some subset of diseases and by making numeric approximations.

Lotfi Zadeh, the inventor of both Fuzzy Logic and Possibility theory is not a native English speaker, and I have always thought that the name "possibility theory" is unfortunate, since in English usage we think of possibility as binary, i.e. possible or impossible, but we do not consider comparative possibilities. I have always thought that "plausibility theory" might have been a better choice, and you might find it easier to substitute plausibility for possibility whenever it is mentioned in the text.

A possibility theoretic analysis of an uncertain system precedes by considering what is possible (or plausible) rather than what is likely. Clearly when building a nuclear power station, a system of laws or a contract a possibilistic analysis is to be preferred.

The probability of two independent events occurring is the product of their individual probabilities, which are all between 0 and 1. So calculating with probabilities can involve some very small numbers and numerical underflow is a problem that has to be addressed.

Possibilities are also between 0 and 1, but the possibility of two independent events occurring is the mathematical minimum of the two, or of a larger set. This makes calculating with fuzzy logic mathematically very tractable.

Another example of this difference in tractability is perhaps best given by an example. A few years ago I worked with a Formula 1 racing company. They had a modelling system for best determining when to bring a driver into the pits, and how many pit stops should be used over the race.

At this time the cars were also refuelled during pit stops.

The variables were the position of the driver on the track, which was uncertain due to telemetry, how much fuel, also uncertain, tyre wear, also uncertain, the position of other drivers, even more uncertain, and other things like the probability of rain, track temperature etc.

The team modelled all these things in the standard way using random number generators with the appropriate distributions around each variable, and they used Monte Carlo simulation to create a model of all the possible outcomes. Monte Carlo simulation involves choosing a set of random numbers and running the simulation, choosing another set and running again, and so on. The more variables you had the more times you had to run the simulation, and this company were running thousands of simulations to create one set of predicted results. This slowed down decision making dramatically even though the process was automated.

I managed to show that by replacing the random distributions with fuzzy numbers the calculations could be generated in a single pass.

Unfortunately, the team ran out of money before we could try this in anger, but this is still a powerful example of how much more tractable Fuzzy Logic and Possibility Theory are.

Forms and Darl

At first glance it may not seem obvious what forms/questionnaires have to do with Darl, and the logic behind the product Darl Forms.

A range of online products exist such as Survey Monkey that enable you to create simple forms and questionnaires. They have a crude ability to influence the flow of the questions, in that it is possible to set up some conditions on questions, so if the user answers "x" to question "y" you don't ask question "z".

We are not trying to compete with these products. Instead there are a large set of applications for businesses and government that are not being served.

Imagine if you owned a bank wishing to launch a new mortgage product. Assuming you have the money and can attract the customers you have one major task left in deciding which of these customers to lend to. After the crash of 2008 this is no longer just about risk profiles, but also large amounts of legislation and compliance rules, as well as those risk profiles determined by the banks risk team.

So, either via a web site, or a tool running on an agent's desk, you want to both collect all the data you need from a customer, and perform the analysis of the data to determine if they get the loan or not.

Now the clue to the use of Darl here is that all these compliance and business requirements are expressed as rules.

So you could create a Darl version of everything, perhaps breaking things up into different rule sets for risk, business rules and legislative compliance so it's easy to isolate what to change if any of those elements change, as they surely will.

So using Darl online you could collect all the data and pass it through the rule sets and get a loan /no loan decision.

But Darl Forms goes much further. If you were using a web site you might want to ask only a few questions at a time, and there might be some questions that are deal breakers. For instance, your bank might not lend on condominiums, but only houses. If so you want to ask this question towards the start.

Darl Forms takes the Darl rule sets you've generated and effectively runs them backwards to work out what the most salient inputs are. These are generally inputs that are the most depended on in the rules.

The inputs are ranked by salience, and the most salient asked first. You can set the number of inputs to ask at a time, and each time a new set of inputs are filled in by the client Darl Forms checks what it still needs to know and adjusts the list.

The client is therefore asked only the minimum of questions, and if they fail the process they are told immediately.

Now even this is not the whole story. We need to define the questions asked, the text displayed back to the user when the results are processed, the form of data capture of inputs and the form of display of outputs. We also need to pass the whole set of completed data to the bank's internal systems.

Darl Forms enables you to control input and output formatting online in a way generic to multiple media types and to set the question text in any language.

If you use the REST interfaces then the report data is available in the final REST interaction of a questionnaire, and if you use our API Apps within the Microsoft Azure Logic App scheme you can trigger other actions when a questionnaire is complete.

The Darl Forms API app creates a web interface for asking questions, or you can use the REST services with any of a range of web site technologies, such as ASP.Net, PhP, etc.

Using Darl Converse and Logic Apps you can even ask questions as an exchange of emails or instant messages.

DARL®

Doctor **A**ndy's **R**ule **L**anguage (pronounced like Darryl) is a computer language intended to encode knowledge as fuzzy logic rules. It is an extremely simple language, and designed to be used with little training. It is intended to be a simple way to represent business or professional knowledge of both logical and numeric kinds, while permitting the representation and processing of various kinds of uncertainty.

Darl is a semi-interpreted language, and both an editor and interpreter are available as web services to be built into web connected applications.

Uniquely, Darl is not only designed so that humans can create representations of knowledge; Darl code can also be created automatically by the processes of data mining, machine learning and machine optimization.

Basic elements of a DARL program

There are a few simple elements to a DARL program.

Rule sets

Analogous to classes in other languages, rule sets are collections of rules that perform a specific purpose. They are functional blocks that do something, calculate something or decide something. A rule set is itself composed of four types of elements

Inputs

These are definitions of the values to be provided to a rule set. They specify a name, used in the rules, a type: numeric, categorical or textual, and extra information like categories or fuzzy sets.

Outputs

These are definitions of the values the rule set will generate. Like inputs, these have names used in the rules, they have types (numeric or categorical), and they have the same extra information.

Constants

These are numeric or string constants used in the rules. DARL makes users define them separately rather than in the rules, so that they can be easily maintained.

Rules

A single rule is of the form *if* <conditions> *then* <output name> *will be* <new output state>;.

Conditions can be arbitrarily complicated, involve inputs, other outputs, logical comparisons, numeric comparisons or numeric expression.

Wiring

A piece of DARL code can contain just one rule set or several. If several, then it is possible to wire these individual rule sets together.

Like integrated circuits in a circuit diagram or schematic, rule set outputs can be wired to other inputs, or to edge connectors to communicate with the outside world.

Organizing Data Flow in Darl

Conventional expert systems spend a lot of their run time working out what gets affected internally by each change to external or internal "facts". Thus, with a conventional expert system, every time you supply a new fact the amount of processing that will be required is indeterminate.

The DARL compiler automatically works out dependencies at the editing stage, and informs the user if they have accidentally coded a circular dependency. The DARL interpreter therefore works out which rules have to be processed in what order, and the order in which rule sets need to be processed automatically.

The DARL Editor

A full suite of editing tools is supplied online to enable users to create Darl online, to test it and to add the formatting and texts needed for questionnaires based on Darl Forms.

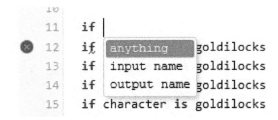

Figure 3, The DARL editor

The Darl editor is an on-line editor especially adapted for the Darl language. It contains a linter that checks the text you give for grammar errors as you type and a suggestion engine that offers the appropriate Darl keywords.

Figure 4, intelligent suggestions

As you type suggested text is created, and the location of any grammar errors are indicated by the red icon to the left, and a red underline beneath the location of the first error.

The linter uses the same compiler as the runtime processor, so a Darl file without errors will be grammatically correct.

By hovering over the underlined text you can see the details of the error.

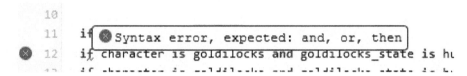

Figure 5, syntax error tagging

You can freely copy text into and out of the editor.

Selecting "Save Changes" will save the most recent copy of the text and return you to the project list page, whereas "Back to List" will do the same without saving changes.

The ☐Form Format Editor

There are several aspects of the display of forms that can be modified using this editor. The page shows lists of the inputs and outputs and permits the user to choose the default number of questions to be shown at a time.

Figure 6, the form format editor

Every time you save the Darl code the associated Format and text files are updates to reflect any changes in the inputs or outputs.

Not all I/O and type combinations are editable. Categorical inputs are always displayed as drop down selections, but numeric and textual inputs as well as all output types have editable attributes.

Numeric inputs

Edit input format

Input Format

Name	porridge_temp
Type	numeric
Show sets	☐
Maximum value	Infinity
Minimum value	-Infinity

Save

Back to List

Figure 7, editing an input

There are two display possibilities with numeric inputs.

Text box with range

If "Show sets" is not selected a text box with range checking will be displayed to the user of the questionnaire. The initial values shown are derived from the range of the variable in any fuzzy sets defined. Change these to practical vales. A warning message will be shown if the user puts in a non-numeric value, or one outside these bounds.

Drop down list with set names

Sometimes, as in asking end-users about their impressions of something, fuzzy terminology is more useful than a numeric value. If you select "Show sets" the set names - or text values you choose to override them in the text page - will be displayed in a drop down box. When the runtime processor evaluates such inputs it replaces the value put into the system with the set definition interpreted as a fuzzy number.

Textual inputs

Edit input format

Input Format

Name	email
Type	textual
Maximum length	0
Regular expression	^([\w\.\-]+)@([\w\-]+)((\.(\w){2,3})+)$

Save

Back to List

Figure 8, editing textual inputs

Textual inputs are always displayed as text edit boxes.

You can set two constraints: the maximum length in characters (0 is treated as no constraint) and a regular expression limiting the input format. The example shows a regular expression accepting only valid email addresses.

Outputs

The inferred results of a form can be shown to the end user at the completion of a form, or hidden. Furthermore, since we use a fuzzy logic inference engine to create the results, we can just return the central or dominant result, or supply uncertainty information. both kinds of outputs have *Hide* and *Uncertainty* select boxes to decide if the output is shown to the end user and if the uncertainty information should be displayed.

Categorical outputs

Edit output format

Output Format

Name	suggestedPage
Type	categorical
Hide	☐
Uncertainty	☑
Display type	Link ▾

Save

Back to List

Figure 9, editing output formats

The only modifiable property other than hidden and uncertainty is whether the result is displayed in the form of a link or as simple text. The text and link format can be set using the text page.

Numeric outputs

Edit output format

Output Format

Name	TOTAL_TAX
Type	numeric
Hide	☐
Uncertainty	☐
Display type	Score bar / Text
Bar color	
Bar max val.	0
Bar min val.	10000
Val. format	0.00

Save

Back to List

Figure 10, editing numeric output formats.

Numeric outputs can be displayed either as text or as score bars. Use the Display Type to select one or other. If Score bar is selected the inputs Bar color, Bar max val and Bar Min val are used to format the score bar.

- Bar color requires a standard RGB value in the format #RRGGBBYY.
- Bar min val requires a numeric value used to determine the minimum value of the bar.

- Bar max val requires a numeric value used to determine the minimum value of the bar.

if Text is selected as the display type a simple textual output is created, formatted according to the format given.

The form text editor

All the text values shown to the user are editable and can be displayed in a variety of languages. The text editor enables you to set these values and the language variants displayed based on the end-users browser language preferences. The initial values given are the names used in the Darl code.

Category and set names

You can override the values shown in drop down boxes. The initial values of these are the values given in the Darl code, and they are identified using the name of the input or output, a "." and the name of the category or set.

Figure 11, editing form text

The above illustrates how to edit the displayed text.

The *Fields in form* drop down holds the names of all the editable fields in the form. The default language is the English text. The language drop-down contains all the two letter ISO languages.

General formatting inputs

All forms are supplied with three general text fields, which will be displayed as headers in the questionnaire.

- *Format.preamble* is displayed at the top of the questionnaire.
- *Format.questionHeader* is displayed above each set of questions.
- *Format.resultHeader* is displayed above the results.

☐ The project page

The project page is accessible via the main menu under the *Editing* tab. It contains a section where you can add a new project with a choice of two types (Several more will be added in the near future.).

Add a new project

project name

goldilocks

project type

DARL source only

Create project

Figure 12, creating a new project

The project list shows a paged and sortable subset of your projects. Depending on the type various actions are available to permit editing and testing of your projects.

Figure 13, editing and testing existing projects

Columns are sortable and filterable. The Map ID column contains the id of that project, which is used with the API app to set the project.

34

Exploiting DARL

Once a piece of knowledge is encapsulated in rules it can be used via the DARL interpreter.

Straight through evaluation

In many applications all the information required is immediately available. In this case the Darl interpreter can be supplied with the values of each input, and the *Evaluate* function can be called. The Interpreter will immediately respond with the calculated/inferred values of the rule outputs

Questionnaire evaluation

This facility is used in our range of Microsoft Azure API apps. The interpreter analyses the rule set and determines which inputs are most pivotal in deciding the outputs. It ranks the inputs in this order. An external application can then request "n" inputs, where n is a small integer, and these will be returned complete with question text and formatting information. The external application returns the users responses to those n questions, and a further n are requested. If an input is no longer required because it has been made redundant by a previous input's response, then it is taken off the list.

In this "questionnaire mode" the fastest path is taken to getting a result.

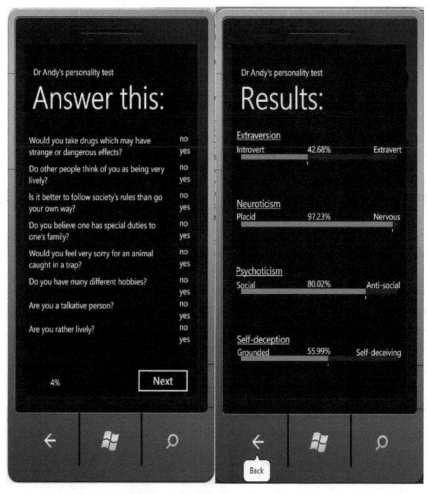

Figure 14, A windows phone app using the REST services

An example of questionnaire evaluation on Windows phone 7.

DARL and uncertainty

The DARL interpreter handles uncertainty in several ways, and this ability is one of the most important features of DARL.

Fuzzy numbers

Often the actual value of an input is not known. The user may know only that it is between two bounds, or there may be more information that permits the creation of a sort of distribution.

The DARL interpreter has a very simple interface that makes the inputting of fuzzy numbers simple.

If there is uncertainty, more than one number can be given for a particular input. These numbers must be in ascending order.

Two values are interpreted as an interval, 3 as a triangular fuzzy number and 4 as a trapezoidal fuzzy number. Representation schemes can be created for higher order fuzziness along the same lines.

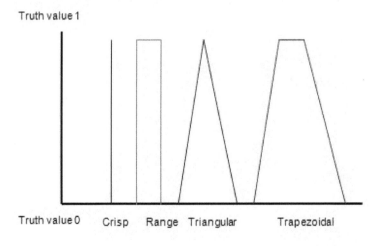

Figure 15, fuzzy set types

Fuzzy categories

It is possible, for a categorical input, to give more than one category, and to apply a confidence figure for each category.

Uncertain rules

Each rule in a DARL rule set can be given a confidence value. This represents the degree of plausibility associated with that rule. When a more plausible rule fires it has the effect of suppressing less plausible rules. The machine generation systems make heavy use of this facility.

Uncertain results

In many cases the results generated by rule evaluation have no uncertainty. However, where fuzzy categories, fuzzy numbers or rule confidences < 1 have been given as input to the interpreter, the results may be uncertain. In this case the output data for each output consists of the inferred value or category, a confidence figure, and either, for numeric outputs a fuzzy number as above, or a list of categories in descending confidence order, each with their individual confidence.

Concatenating uncertainty

Where a DARL code file contains more than one rule set, then by default all of the uncertainty information is passed from outputs to inputs within the evaluation.

Rule set testing

Rule sets can be tested online.

Figure 16, testing rule sets and forms

In the first image a rule set is tested by supplying all the required data and evaluating all at once. In the second, for Darl Forms, a full simulation of the form is provided.

Creating DARL code through machine learning / data mining

"Data mining" is a general term for gaining insights from data. The subject is governed by two areas of theory: statistics and artificial intelligence. Scientio takes an AI approach to data mining, and considers data mining to be an example of various kinds of machine learning.

So various kinds of statistical regression map onto the AI idea of "supervised learning", forms of clustering map on to "unsupervised learning" and optimization maps onto "learning with a critic".

Scientio has created various algorithms to implement each kind of machine learning.

Uniquely, these algorithms have been designed to <u>create DARL code directly.</u>

So, it is possible to create functional rule sets directly from data.

To give a simple example, if you were a bank or similar lender, and in possession of a set of loan applications from existing customers, and you also had the payment records associated with each loan, you could create a DARL rule set directly from the data that you could use to decide on future loan applications.

Supervised Learning

Supervised learning is learning by example. To use this method many examples of input and output data must be found, which will be used as a training set for the learning algorithm.

Data items that are used in data mining can be thought of as falling into three types: Numeric, categorical and textual.

Numeric data

Data items can contain real numbers, integers, dates and times. Our supervised learning algorithm looks at the range and density of these values over the supplied data set, and assigns fuzzy sets to them. The number of fuzzy sets is the only value that needs to be externally controlled.

40

Categorical data

These data items are intended to represent categories, such as "male, female" or "single, married, separated, divorced". Note that sometimes numbers are used for categories in data sets. If a data item is marked categorical, then our algorithm will search for all the categories present in the data set.

Textual data

Textual data can be mined using our text mining or concept mining technologies, which are outside the scope of this document.

Hierarchical data

If the training data source is tree shaped, for instance XML, the algorithm can mine the structure of the document. It can base this on the *Arity* of nodes in the document, i.e. the count of nodes at a particular place in the data tree, and the *Presence* of nodes, i.e. whether or not a particular kind of node exists.

Rule generation

To perform supervised learning, the user specifies some basic information about the recurring data items in the data, how to find them, and their types. He or she selects one data item to be predicted. This will become the output of the rule set, the others will be inputs. The supervised learning algorithm then performs initial processing on the data, fills in fuzzy sets and categories, randomly associates data rows into either training or test rows, generates a rule set based on the training set, and tests performance.

The actual rule generation proceeds by creating a fuzzy logic decision tree, and then reads this back from leaf to root to create rules.

Key characteristics

No numeric bias

Unlike many wholly numeric learning algorithms, like Support Vector Machines and Neural Nets, our algorithm does not have a bias towards numeric variables and handles all kinds of variables and mixtures thereof equally.

Resistance to overtraining

All learning algorithms, and some statistical techniques have a tendency to "overlearn"; that is to create a solution that is accurate on the source it was created with, but that generalizes poorly. Our algorithm has inbuilt techniques to prevent this.

Intelligibility
The resulting models are intelligible to humans. Being expressed in terms of "if.. then..." rules and using fuzzy set terms like "small", "medium" and "large", the created rules can be understood by non-technical personnel. This compares very favourably to SVM and neural nets. In these cases the models are extremely hard for the non-technical to understand.

Unsupervised learning
This behaves very much as supervised learning, except that no output is provided in the training data. The unsupervised learning algorithm must generate one itself. This is performed using the AI version of clustering.

Learning with a critic / Reinforcement learning
This algorithm permits machine optimization of or generation of rule sets. In many real world systems there may be a missing functional block, or that block may perform poorly. Sometimes an analytic solution does not exist to fill in the missing block, as with NP complete problems, or there is insufficient information to select an analytic solution.

For instance, in the case of financial program trading, a trading algorithm may exist that has a poor choice of parameters. Using a simulated trading system and historical data the value of these parameters can be optimized. Similarly, a new trading algorithm may be sought, and this can be created from scratch using genetic processes.

Scientio can offer two learning algorithms useful in this case. For an existing rule set constants can be optimized, and where no solution exists a solution can be generated using Genetic Programming.

To make use of these two algorithms there must be a simulation of the rest of the system available, so that the DARL solutions can be tested, and there must be a measure of performance, selected so that even the poorest performers have some score, and if A performs better than B, the score of A is > the score of B. Dr Andy's learning with a critic algorithms will continually generate new solutions, improving them based on the score provided, until an agreed performance level or runtime limit is met.

As in supervised learning, the rule sets generated are intelligible to non-technical personnel.

Integrating machine generated code

Machine generated DARL code is just like the code you would write by hand. It can be integrated into a larger piece of DARL code as a rule set, and so you can have a solution that has human generated and machine generated elements.

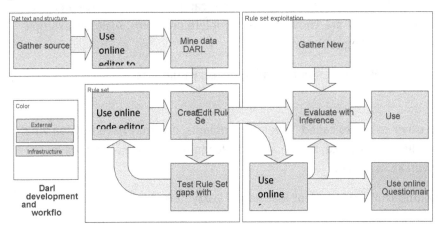

Figure 17, General DARL workflow

Application areas for Fuzzy Rules

Computer science is mostly concerned with "analytic" solutions to problems. This means finding an algorithm that performs some required task accurately, and where more than one algorithm is available, selecting between them.

If there is an obvious analytic solution to your problem, you are unlikely to want to use Fuzzy Rules. There are several circumstances where Dr Andy's technology can help:

NP Complete problems

As Gödel showed, not all problems that can be described have analytic solutions. These are known as NP complete problems. A classic example is the "travelling salesman" problem.

Solutions: Reinforcement learning of Fuzzy Rule sets.

Inverse problems

In other cases, so called "inverse" problems, one may have no idea what a solution looks like, but be able to recognize one by how it behaves, if given an example.

Solutions: Reinforcement learning of Fuzzy Rule sets.

Uncertain and noisy problem definitions

There may be large amounts of uncertainty associated with the required solution, the input data may be vague or noisy, and the outputs may be poorly defined.

Solutions: Supervised learning of Fuzzy Rule sets.

Solution only known to an expert

The solution may only be embodied in the experience of an expert, who can only explain how he performs his task in vague human, as opposed to computer, terms.

Solutions: Manual creation of Fuzzy Rule sets.

Non-stationary problems

The requirements for a solution may be continually changing, for instance in business and finance, and an analytic solution would become out of date by the time it was written.

Solutions: Supervised learning of Fuzzy Rule sets.

Needless to say, some of the most interesting problems fall into the last cases. Our system supplies a set of tools to attack such problems.

Sometimes our tools can be used to find a solution to one of the problem types above, most often an inverse problem, which can then later be replaced with an analytic solution. This has occurred with medical diagnosis solutions we have provided, for instance.

What it costs

Use of the Darl web services is free for rate-limited usage. The rate limit is set at no more than 100 ruleset evaluations per minute, and no more than 1000 per week. It is possible to run an experimental set up using Darl without paying anything at all. To lift the limit users must subscribe to the "unlimited" subscription which costs a minimum of $50 per month. Each rule set evaluation is charged at a small fee, currently 1 cent, per usage. Users will be billed the greater of $50 and the previous month's usage fees.

Example Darl Form: A Personality Test

The intention of this example is to show how a quite complicated, and mostly numeric, process can be turned into a functioning questionnaire using DARL.

The source for this is a personality test created by the Anglo-German psychologist Hans Eysenck et alia in 1985. You can find the original paper at http://www.pbarrett.net/publications/EPQR_1985_paper.pdf.

This test asks the user 100 questions to which the answers are yes or no. Each question is related to one of four personality traits, and is marked as either positively affecting the score for that trait, or negatively affecting the score.

Like many early personality tests, this is configured so that a tester can calculate the results by hand.

The one hundred questions are asked, and then for each trait, and depending on the polarity of the question, one is added to the sum for the trait the question relates to for either a yes or a no answer as expected, or zero otherwise.

At the end of this process we have 4 raw totals for each trait.

A further two questions are asked giving the user's age and gender. Professor Eysenck has modelled the distributions of these traits for 6 age bands between 16 and 70 and both genders, and assumed they are Gaussians, defined by a central value and standard deviation. There are thus 12 distributions for each trait. The manual tester would have had these supplied as look up tables in the back of a testing manual.

The end result is a set of four percentile values, defining the user's position in the general population for his or her age group and gender.

The traits are labelled psychoticism (P), neuroticism (N), extroversion (E) and lying (L).

The following diagram shows the process:

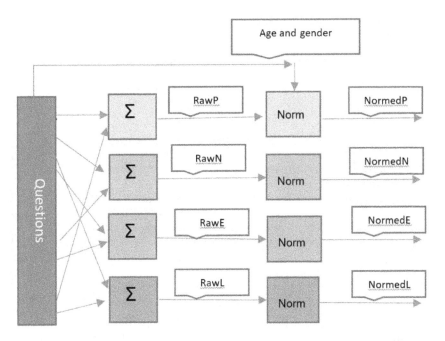

Figure 18, the process of scoring the personality test

Creating the rule set

In order to model this process in Darl, we will need, as usual, a set of input definitions, a set of output definitions, any constants we need and the rules themselves.

The inputs pose a small problem. The user is presented with yes/no alternatives, but the calculations require numeric values. Darl has a facility to treat a numeric input as a categorical one for user interface purposes if a set of fuzzy sets is defined. Thus, for a numeric input, you might define sets "small", "medium" and "large" and either ask for a numeric value, which could be converted to a degree of truth of set membership, or you can pass the set names, in which case the appropriate set, treated as a fuzzy number is passed on to the internal processing.

In this case we choose the latter, but limit the sets to the values "0" or "1" appropriately.

The first 8 input definitions look like this:

```
4    input numeric item1  {{no , 0.000, 0.000, 0.000}, {yes , 1.000, 1.000, 1.000}};
5    input numeric item2  {{no , 1.000, 1.000, 1.000}, {yes , 0.000, 0.000, 0.000}};
6    input numeric item3  {{no , 0.000, 0.000, 0.000}, {yes , 1.000, 1.000, 1.000}};
7    input numeric item4  {{no , 1.000, 1.000, 1.000}, {yes , 0.000, 0.000, 0.000}};
8    input numeric item5  {{no , 1.000, 1.000, 1.000}, {yes , 0.000, 0.000, 0.000}};
9    input numeric item6  {{no , 0.000, 0.000, 0.000}, {yes , 1.000, 1.000, 1.000}};
10   input numeric item7  {{no , 1.000, 1.000, 1.000}, {yes , 0.000, 0.000, 0.000}};
11   input numeric item8  {{no , 0.000, 0.000, 0.000}, {yes , 1.000, 1.000, 1.000}};
```

Figure 19, Personality test inputs

There are another 92 of these.

There are also definitions for Age and Gender:

```
104    input numeric Age    {{medium , 16.000, 45.000, 70.000}};
105    input categorical Gender   {male, female};
```

Figure 20, more personality test inputs

In this instance we've created a single fuzzy set for Age. This set will be used to set the default range of the variable for validation purposes. Depending on the UI you use to present the form, validation mechanisms can limit the input to somewhere in this range.

The outputs are much simpler:

```
106    //Output definitions
107    output numeric RawP;
108    output numeric RawE;
109    output numeric RawN;
110    output numeric RawL;
111    output numeric NormedP;
112    output numeric NormedE;
113    output numeric NormedN;
114    output numeric NormedL;
```

Figure 21, personality test outputs

Here we define 4 raw outputs for intermediate values, and 4 final outputs.

The rules will make use of numerical constants. Each distribution has two values, and there are 6 x 2 x 4, so 96 values in total.

Here are the first few:

```
115    //numeric constant definitions
116    constant PAveMale16_20 9.57;
117    constant PSDMale16_20 5.26;
118    constant PAveMale21_30 8.65;
119    constant PSDMale21_30 4.56;
120    constant PAveMale31_40 6.69;
121    constant PSDMale31_40 3.58;
122    constant PAveMale41_50 7.00;
123    constant PSDMale41_50 4.65;
124    constant PAveMale51_60 5.28;
125    constant PSDMale51_60 3.59;
126    constant PAveMale61_70 4.87;
127    constant PSDMale61_70 3.55;
128    constant PAveFemale16_20 7.06;
129    constant PSDFemale16_20 4.11;
```

Figure 22, personality test constants

We've just adopted a simple naming convention for the averages and standard deviations.

Finally, we have the rules.

The raw output values are fairly simple:

```
    if anything then RawE will be sum( item1 , item6 , item11
, item16 , item20 , item28 , item36 , item40 , item45 ,
item51 , item55 , item58 , item61 , item63 , item67 , item69
, item72 , item78 , item90 , item94 , item24 , item33 ,
item47 ) confidence 1.00;

    if anything then RawP will be sum( item25 , item29 ,
item30 , item34 , item37 , item42 , item48 , item50 , item56
, item73 , item75 , item91 , item95 , item2 , item5 , item7 ,
item9 , item12 , item14 , item18 , item21 , item41 , item54 ,
item59 , item64 , item68 , item79 , item81 , item85 , item88
, item96 , item99 ) confidence 1.00;

    if anything then RawN will be sum( item3 , item8 , item13
, item17 , item22 , item26 , item31 , item35 , item38 ,
item43 , item46 , item52 , item60 , item65 , item70 , item74
, item76 , item80 , item83 , item84 , item87 , item92 ,
item97 , item100 ) confidence 1.00;
```

```
    if anything then RawL will be sum( item15 , item23 ,
item39 , item62 , item86 , item98 , item4 , item10 , item19 ,
item27 , item32 , item44 , item49 , item53 , item57 , item66
, item71 , item77 , item82 , item89 , item93 ) confidence
1.00;
```

There are no conditions to be met before the values are calculated, so the rules start with "if anything" and the numeric outputs are set to the sum of the appropriate outputs. Using this mechanism, we can just pick the questions that relate to this trait and sum them.

So now we need to perform the final calculation of the percentiles for the "normed" outputs.

There are 6 age ranges, 2 genders and 4 traits, so we need 48 rules. The first few look like this:

```
    if Age is >= 16 and Age is < 21 and Gender is male then
NormedP will be 100 * normprob( ( RawP - PAveMale16_20 ) /
PSDMale16_20 ) confidence 1.00;

    if Age is > 20 and Age is < 31 and Gender is male then
NormedP will be 100 * normprob( ( RawP - PAveMale21_30 ) /
PSDMale21_30 ) confidence 1.00;

    if Age is > 30 and Age is < 41 and Gender is male then
NormedP will be 100 * normprob( ( RawP - PAveMale31_40 ) /
PSDMale31_40 ) confidence 1.00;

    if Age is > 40 and Age is < 51 and Gender is male then
NormedP will be 100 * normprob( ( RawP - PAveMale41_50 ) /
PSDMale41_50 ) confidence 1.00;

    if Age is > 50 and Age is < 61 and Gender is male then
NormedP will be 100 * normprob( ( RawP - PAveMale51_60 ) /
PSDMale51_60 ) confidence 1.00;

    if Age is > 60 and Age is < 71 and Gender is male then
NormedP will be 100 * normprob( ( RawP - PAveMale61_70 ) /
PSDMale61_70 ) confidence 1.00;

    if Age is >= 16 and Age is < 21 and Gender is female then
NormedP will be 100 * normprob( ( RawP - PAveFemale16_20 ) /
PSDFemale16_20 ) confidence 1.00;

    if Age is > 20 and Age is < 31 and Gender is female then
NormedP will be 100 * normprob( ( RawP - PAveFemale21_30 ) /
PSDFemale21_30 ) confidence 1.00;
```

```
    if Age is > 30 and Age is < 41 and Gender is female then
NormedP will be 100 * normprob( ( RawP - PAveFemale31_40 ) /
PSDFemale31_40 ) confidence 1.00;

    if Age is > 40 and Age is < 51 and Gender is female then
NormedP will be 100 * normprob( ( RawP - PAveFemale41_50 ) /
PSDFemale41_50 ) confidence 1.00;

    if Age is > 50 and Age is < 61 and Gender is female then
NormedP will be 100 * normprob( ( RawP - PAveFemale51_60 ) /
PSDFemale51_60 ) confidence 1.00;

    if Age is > 60 and Age is < 71 and Gender is female then
NormedP will be 100 * normprob( ( RawP - PAveFemale61_70 ) /
PSDFemale61_70 ) confidence 1.00;
```

Here we are using numeric comparisons to detect the range, but we might also have created more fuzzy sets on the Age. So, for instance, if we had a fuzzy set {"16_20",16,20} defined for age we could have written:

If age is 16_20 and Gender is male...

The numerical calculations of NormedP just pick the appropriate constants and scale the values entered into the built in function "normprob" appropriately.

Formatting the presentation

You can set the form formatting by selecting the "Format" button on the project page.

The inputs look like this.

Inputs

	Name	Type	▼ Show sets	Min range	Max range	Increment	Max length	Reg. expression
Edit	item1	numeric	True	0	1	0		
Edit	item2	numeric	True	0	1	0		
Edit	item3	numeric	True	0	1	0		
Edit	item4	numeric	True	0	1	0		
Edit	item5	numeric	True	0	1	0		
Edit	item6	numeric	True	0	1	0		
Edit	item7	numeric	True	0	1	0		
Edit	item8	numeric	True	0	1	0		
Edit	item9	numeric	True	0	1	0		
Edit	item10	numeric	True	0	1	0		

1 2 3 ... 11 »

Figure 23, Form format personality test inputs

These inputs have been auto generated from the rule set, and all additions and changes to the number of them have to occur there. In this instance there is only one thing we need to change for the inputs which is the "show sets" field. If this is true then the defined sets are displayed as a set of choices, if false the input will normally be displayed as an edit box restricted to numbers with range validation – if the media you choose supports this.

Edit the input format

Name	item1
Type	numeric
Show sets	☑
Maximum value	1
Minimum value	0

Save

Figure 24, editing a form format input

Edit each input to show sets.

Now we need to set up the formatting of the outputs.

Outputs

	Name	Type	▼ Hide	Show uncertainty	Val. format	Display type	Bar min	Bar max
Edit	RawP	numeric	True	False		Text		
Edit	RawE	numeric	True	False		Text		
Edit	RawN	numeric	True	False		Text		
Edit	RawL	numeric	True	False		Text		
Edit	NormedL	numeric	False	False		ScoreBar	0	100
Edit	NormedE	numeric	False	False		ScoreBar	0	100
Edit	NormedN	numeric	False	False		ScoreBar	0	100
Edit	NormedP	numeric	False	False		ScoreBar	0	100

Default questions | 5 | Change

Figure 25, , Form Format personality test outputs

There are two things to change. We want the values of RawP, RawE, RawN and RawL to be hidden from the user.

We do this by editing those inputs and setting "hide" to true.

52

Edit the output format

Figure 26, editing a personality test output

For the four outputs that are visible to the user, we could just display the percentiles as numbers, but it's more fun to present them as horizontal score bars. This is performed like this:

Edit the output format

Figure 27, editing a personality test score bar.

Here we've selected a score bar as the output format, given it a color, and set the range to 0-100.

Providing the text

The text can be changed on everything, and provided in as many languages as you like. If the medium you choose to display the form supports language selection you can provide all the text in the appropriate language. Thus one questionnaire can apply to all the locations your company serves.

The standard text editor looks like this:

Edit form text
Form text and language support

Figure 28, editing the text of the personality test

The default language is English for the time being.

The "fields in form "drop-down has all the text items that can be edited.

Fields in form

Age
Format.preamble
Format.questionHeader
Format.resultHeader
Gender
Gender.female
Gender.male
item1
item10
item100
item11
item12
item13
item14
item15
item16
item17
item18
item19
item2
item20
item21
item22
item23
item24
item25
item26
item27
item28

Figure 29, text selections for the personality test 1

Where an input name is shown, selecting that field will allow you to edit the question associated with the input. The choices for categorical inputs or set names if used are displayed as <input name>.<category name>. So above you can edit the text shown for the female gender selection.

The Format values are built ins that are provided to display at the top of the form. The Format.preamble value is provided at the top of every screen,

The Format.questionHeader is displayed normally below this for questions, and the Format.resultHeader is displayed above the results.

At the bottom of the list we have the output fields:

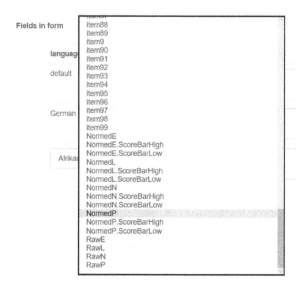

Figure 30, text selections for the personality test 2

The scoreBarHigh and scoreBarLow texts are displayed to the right and the left of the score bar respectively.

Let's see how this looks in practice. You can view and test the form using the "Form test" button on the project page.

This is the first page:

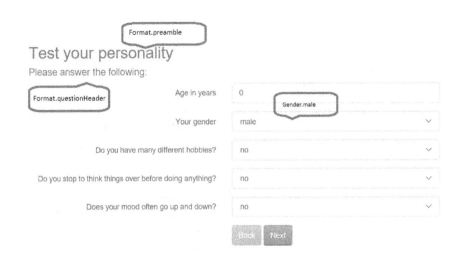

Figure 31, first page of the personality test.

Since there are 100 questions there are multiple screens between, but the last looks like this:

Figure 32, last page of the personality test.

Using the data collected

Dr Andy's IP considers your data to be private, so none of the values returned or inferred are stored by us. However, all of the data items collected and the inferred results, whether hidden or not, are returned with the final REST response as a name-value pair list in the "values" field.

If you use our API app then completion of the form as a trigger to the enclosing Logic App, and the values are passed on as JSON to the other processes.

Integration with Microsoft Azure

No technology will have much success with developers unless integration and testing is simple.

Furthermore, as well as "front end" user centric applications, this technology is also useful in "back end" applications such as back office functionality where inferences or complex business rules must be followed.

Microsoft has attacked the back end marketplace with API apps and Logic Apps. The former are REST modules with standardised interfaces hosted on Azure, and the latter is a new framework for solving sequential processing tasks by composing sets of API apps, using a visual environment.

All our products are hosted on Azure. We have also created several open source API apps that can be used inside Logic apps to perform various functions.

Clearly our ability to add inference to a process is very important, but only part of the story. Using Logic Apps, you can, for instance, create a form that triggers further processing – maybe an application process – when the form is completed.

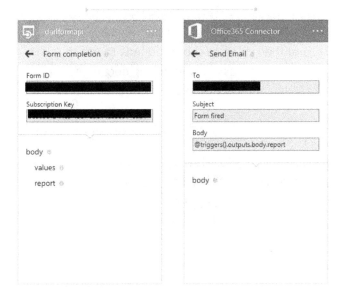

Figure 33, A simple logic app using DARL

The above shows a Logic app using a Darl forms API app triggering another to send an email when a form is completed containing the form results.

☐

An end to end tutorial using Microsoft API Apps

This tutorial will show you first how to create a Darl file for a simple logical inference task, and then go on to show you how to use this with the Api apps, by adding project types and supporting documents. After you've read this you can view the Darl Converse tutorial which relies on this tutorial.

Example inference task

To choose something simple and general let's pick a nursery story that everyone in the English speaking world will have come across, the story of Goldilocks and the three bears. Trivial as this story might seem, to model the actions of the characters we need both numeric and categorical values. The story contains fuzzy linguistic variables like "too hot", "too cold", "too big", etc. so we can make use of fuzzy sets.

Creating a project

Setting up a Darl or DarlForms app takes place on two sites, the Azure portal and the docandys site. Go to the latter first, and register for a new account, or sign in if you have already.

Then go to the "Editing" menu item and create a new project by making the following changes:

Add a new project

project name

goldilocks

project type

DARL source only

Create project

Figure 34, tutorial creating a project

Select "Create Project".

The resulting project will appear in the list below.

| goldilocks | DARL | 7/2/2015 11:36:39 AM | dda2f639-73f8-410f-a95a-af96a9c42c86 | Edit code | Test |

Figure 35, tutorial, the new project

Note that your Map ID will be different from the above. This is the ID that identifies the project and all its elements to the API apps.

Now click on the "Edit Code" button and the Darl edit window will appear.

Darl Ruleset

```
1  ruleset ruleset1
2  {
3  }
4
```

Save changes

Figure 36, tutorial, the empty rule set

Change the name of the ruleset from "ruleset1" to "goldilocks".

The first thing to do is to determine what the inputs and outputs are. The rule set will direct the characters of the story, so we need to have a list of them. So the first thing to do is to create a character input. This contains an array of choices, so is a categorical input. You use these for anything with categories.

```
ruleset goldilocks

{

    input categorical character {goldilocks, mama_bear, papa_bear,
baby_bear};

}
```

Notice that at each stage of editing the editor suggests completion choices, and the left margin contains a red mark to indicate grammar errors. If you hover over the error icon, you will see a description of the error. Note that, like "C" the lines end in semicolons. Names should also obey the "C" rules for names, so no spaces, and can't start with a number.'

The main character has three states, hungry, tired and sleepy. Let's add a categorical input for that.

```
ruleset goldilocks

{

    input categorical character {goldilocks, mama_bear, papa_bear,
baby_bear};

    input categorical goldilocks_state {hungry,tired,sleepy};

}
```

Now, in the story there is porridge that is too hot, too cold, and just right. Let's construct an input for that.

```
ruleset goldilocks

{

    input categorical character {goldilocks, mama_bear, papa_bear,
baby_bear};

    input categorical goldilocks_state {hungry,tired,sleepy};

    input numeric porridge_temp {{too_cold,-
infinity,20,30},{just_right,20,30,40},{too_hot,30,40,Infinity}};

}
```

You can read more about fuzzy sets earlier on in this book, but this describes three fuzzy sets for the input porridge_temp. The example uses metric units throughout, so we're saying that we have a fuzzy set stretching from -infinity to 20 degrees C with degree of truth 1, dropping to degree of truth 0 at 30 for too cold. Just_right is a triangular set going from 20C, peaking at 30C, and returning to zero truth at 40C. Too_hot starts at 30c, raises to 40c for degree of truth 1 and stays there to +infinity. Note that Infinity is case sensitive, and also that, by convention, the sets overlap so that the sum of the degrees of truth add up to one across the domain of the variable.

Let's add similar inputs for chair height, in meters, and bed softness. (The latter holding the Young's modulus of the material.).

```
ruleset goldilocks

{

    input categorical character {goldilocks, mama_bear, papa_bear,
baby_bear};

    input categorical goldilocks_state {hungry,tired,sleepy};

    input numeric porridge_temp {{too_cold,-
Infinity,20,30},{just_right,20,30,40},{too_hot,30,40,Infinity}};

    input numeric chair_height {{too_low,-
Infinity,0.2,0.3},{just_right,0.2,0.3,0.4},{too_high,0.3,0.4,0.5},{muc
h_too_high,0.4,0.5,Infinity}};

    input numeric bed_softness {{too_hard,-Infinity,
90,100},{just_right,90,100,110},{too_soft,100,110,Infinity}};

}
```

So now we need at least one output. Let's make it a set of directions as to what to do next. Let's start with Goldilocks, and we'll look at the bears later.

```
ruleset goldilocks

{

    input categorical character {goldilocks, mama_bear, papa_bear,
baby_bear};

    input categorical goldilocks_state {hungry,tired,sleepy};

    input numeric porridge_temp {{too_cold,-
Infinity,20,30},{just_right,20,30,40},{too_hot,30,40,Infinity}};

    input numeric chair_height {{too_low,-
Infinity,0.2,0.3},{just_right,0.2,0.3,0.4},{too_high,0.3,0.4,0.5},{muc
h_too_high,0.4,0.5,Infinity}};
```

```
  input numeric bed_softness {{too_hard,-Infinity,
90,100},{just_right,90,100,110},{too_soft,100,110,Infinity}};

  output categorical action {try_another_porridge, try_another_chair,
break_chair, try_another_bed, go_to_sleep};

}
```

Now we have inputs and outputs we need some rules:

```
ruleset goldilocks

{

  input categorical character {goldilocks, mama_bear, papa_bear,
baby_bear};

  input categorical goldilocks_state {hungry,tired,sleepy};

  input numeric porridge_temp {{too_cold,-
Infinity,20,30},{just_right,20,30,40},{too_hot,30,40,Infinity}};

  input numeric chair_height {{too_low,-
Infinity,0.2,0.3},{just_right,0.2,0.3,0.4},{too_high,0.3,0.4,0.5},{much
_too_high,0.4,0.5,Infinity}};

  input numeric bed_softness {{too_hard,-Infinity,
90,100},{just_right,90,100,110},{too_soft,100,110,Infinity}};

  output categorical action {try_another_porridge, eat_porridge,
try_another_chair, break_chair, try_another_bed, go_to_sleep};


  if character is goldilocks and goldilocks_state is hungry and
porridge_temp is just_right then action will be eat_porridge;

  if character is goldilocks and goldilocks_state is hungry and not
porridge_temp is just_right then action will be try_another_porridge;

  if character is goldilocks and goldilocks_state is tired and
chair_height is just_right then action will be break_chair;

  if character is goldilocks and goldilocks_state is tired and not
chair_height is just_right then action will be try_another_chair;

  if character is goldilocks and goldilocks_state is sleepy and
bed_softness is just_right then action will be go_to_sleep;
```

```
    if character is goldilocks and goldilocks_state is sleepy and not
bed_softness is just_right then action will be try_another_bed;

}
```

Hopefully these are reasonably clear without too much explanation. Each rule starts with "if", is followed by a bunch of conditions, the word "then", an output name, "will be" and the new state of the output if the rule fires. The conditions use the logical operators "and", "or" and "not". There is also another operator "anything", which makes a rule always succeed. "is" is used to test inputs or outputs used as inputs (this is possible, so long as you don't make loops). The left side of an "is" holds the input or output name, the right side whatever you want to test against. If it's a categorical input or output one of the defined categories can be used, if numeric either a set name or an arithmetic expression.

If you've got a complete ruleset with no compilation errors, then you can test it. Save the edited ruleset and choose "Test" from the "existing projects" table.

Figure 37, tutorial, testing the rule set.

Change the selections to look like the above and select "Test on ruleset".

Figure 38, tutorial, testing the rule set 2.

The action will be as above if you've types in the ruleset properly.

The "Detail" button brings up a pop up window containing uncertainty information:

Figure 39, Tutorial, uncertainty information from testing

Now close the pop up and switch "goldilocks_state" to "tired" and test again. This time the result is empty, because we don't have a value for "chair_height", and the pop up will show the following:

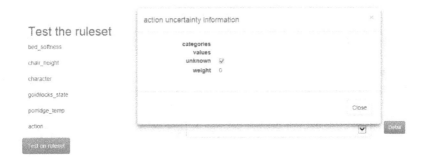

Figure 40, Tutorial, more uncertainty information

The rules for the other characters can be added easily. Note that there's a new input "bear_state", and the list of actions have been extended. The categories are shorthand for "who's been sleeping in my bed?" etc.

```
ruleset goldilocks
{
  input categorical character {goldilocks, mama_bear, papa_bear,
baby_bear};
  input categorical goldilocks_state {hungry,tired,sleepy};
  input categorical bear_state {outside,livingroom,bedroom};
  input numeric porridge_temp {{too_cold,-
Infinity,20,30},{just_right,20,30,40},{too_hot,30,40,Infinity}};
  input numeric chair_height {{too_low,-
Infinity,0.2,0.3},{just_right,0.2,0.3,0.4},{too_high,0.3,0.4,0.5},{much
_too_high,0.4,0.5,Infinity}};
  input numeric bed_softness {{too_hard,-Infinity,
90,100},{just_right,90,100,110},{too_soft,100,110,Infinity}};
  output categorical action {try_another_porridge, eat_porridge,
try_another_chair, break_chair, try_another_bed, go_to_sleep,
say_WBEMP, say_WBEMPA, say_WBSIMC, sayWBSIMCB, say_WBSIMB,
say_WBSIMBST};

  if character is goldilocks and goldilocks_state is hungry and
porridge_temp is just_right then action will be eat_porridge;
  if character is goldilocks and goldilocks_state is hungry and not
porridge_temp is just_right then action will be try_another_porridge;
  if character is goldilocks and goldilocks_state is tired and
chair_height is just_right then action will be break_chair;
  if character is goldilocks and goldilocks_state is tired and not
chair_height is just_right then action will be try_another_chair;
  if character is goldilocks and goldilocks_state is sleepy and
bed_softness is just_right then action will be go_to_sleep;
```

```
    if character is goldilocks and goldilocks_state is sleepy and not
bed_softness is just_right then action will be try_another_bed;
    if character is baby_bear and bear_state is outside then action will
be say_WBEMPA;
    if character is baby_bear and bear_state is livingroom then action
will be say_WBSIMCB;
    if character is baby_bear and bear_state is bedroom then action will
be say_WBSIMBST;
    if character is mama_bear and bear_state is outside then action will
be say_WBEMP;
    if character is mama_bear and bear_state is livingroom then action
will be say_WBSIMC;
    if character is mama_bear and bear_state is bedroom then action will
be say_WBSIMB;
    if character is papa_bear and bear_state is outside then action will
be say_WBEMP;
    if character is papa_bear and bear_state is livingroom then action
will be say_WBSIMC;
    if character is papa_bear and bear_state is bedroom then action will
be say_WBSIMB;
}
```

Creating a form

Create a new project of the type "Darl form" called "goldilocks form" and
copy and paste the previous rule set into the code editor for that form
and save the changes.

Saving the code automatically updates the Format and language
specifications with the inputs and outputs. If you click on the "Edit
Format" button in the project list beside the project, you should see this:

Edit Format

Inputs

	Name	Type	▼ Show sets	Min range	Max range	Increment	Max length	Reg. expression
	character	categorical						
	goldilocks_state	categorical						
	bear_state	categorical						
Edit	porridge_temp	numeric	False	-Infinity	Infinity	0		
Edit	chair_height	numeric	False	-Infinity	Infinity	0		
Edit	bed_softness	numeric	False	-Infinity	Infinity	0		

Outputs

	Name	Type	▼ Hide	Show uncertainty	Val. format	Display type	Bar min	Bar max
Edit	action	categorical	False	False		0		

Default questions [1] [Change]

Figure 41, Tutorial, editing the input formats

The "Edit Format" page allows you to change the display format of the various inputs and outputs. For instance, for numeric inputs you can select "show sets" in which case in the final questionnaire the UI will display a drop down with the set names, rather than require a numeric input. For outputs you can change the way the data is displayed. Numeric outputs can be displayed as bars or as formatted numbers.

We don't need to change anything here.

Now go to the "Edit Texts" page.

Edit form text

Form text and language support

Fields in form	action	▼

language	text	
default	Do this:	[Change]
Afrikaans ▼		[Add]

[Back to List]

Figure 42, Tutorial, editing the texts.

This enables you to set the text associated with each question. The top drop down contains every field that can have text associated.

Note that as well as the default text, which is in English, you can set language variants in any language.

For each text defaults are provided, but in most cases you will want to replace them, especially for other languages.

There are lots of texts to change, but the following is a list of suggested texts.

Name	Text
character	Which character are you?
character.goldilocks	Goldilocks
character.mama_bear	Mama bear
character.papa_bear	Papa bear
character.baby_bear	baby bear
goldilocks_state	How is Goldilocks feeling?
goldilocks_state.hungry	hungry
goldilocks_state.tired	tired
goldilocks_state.sleepy	sleepy
bear_state	Where are the 3 bears?
bear_state.outside	outside of the house

Name	Text
bear_state.livingroom	In the living room
bear_state.bedroom	In the bedroom
porridge_temp	How hot is the porridge (Deg. C)
chair_height	How high is the chair? (M)
bed_softness	How soft is the bed?
action	Do this:
action.try_another_porridge	try another porridge
action.eat_porridge	eat porridge
action.try_another_chair	try another chair
action.break_chair	break chair
action.try_another_bed	try another bed
action.go_to_sleep	go to sleep
action.say_WBEMP	Say "Who's been eating my porridge?"
action.say_WBEMPA	Say "Who's been eating my porridge? And it's all gone!"

Name	Text
action.say_WBSIMC	Say "Who's been sitting in my chair?"
action.sayWBSIMCB	Say "Who's been sitting in my chair? And they've broken it!"
action.say_WBSIMB	Say "Who's been sleeping in my bed?"
action.say_WBSIMBST	Say "Who's been sleeping in my bed? And they're still there!"
Format.preamble	
Format.questionHeader	
Format.resultHeader	

Testing the questionnaire

To test the questionnaire, choose test in the projects list

Figure 43, tutorial, testing the questionnaire

Using the results in a Logic App

We've built a form from scratch, complete with logic, text and formatting. Now we need to use it with a Logic App.

This is quite straightforward, though at the time of writing Logic Apps are not finalized and some details may change.

The two key pieces of information you need are the project Map ID, available in the projects list, and one of your keys available by clicking on your name in the log in and selecting Profile.

Figure 44, tutorial, finding the subscription key

Wiring up a Darl Form in a Logic App

Add a darlformapi to the logic app surface by clicking on the instance in the resource group set of API apps. Add the Map ID and subscription key from above. Then add an Office 365 Connector. (This assumes you have an Office 365 account) When you instantiate the connector you will associate it with your account.

Set the "to address" to your email, and set the subject to "Form fired". Finally link the body to a formatted version of the results from the darlformapi app, available in the report section of the outputs.

by typing

```
@triggers().outputs.body.report
```

This sets the logic app to respond to a push trigger from the app whenever a form is completed, and to email the formatted results to you.

Note that at the time of writing, push triggers are only updated hourly within Azure, so you may have to wait until this starts to work. Until the trigger is loaded the web page will show an error.

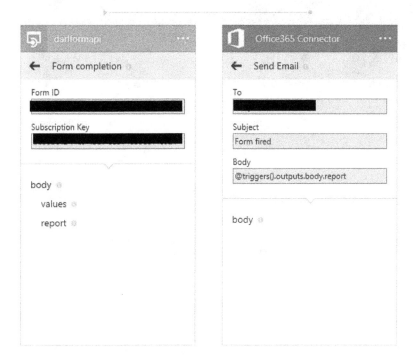

Figure 45, Tutorial, the example Logic App

The final question is the address of the form. This is found in the settings of the Darl form API app.

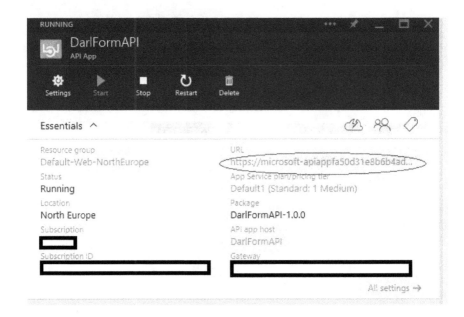

Figure 46, Tutorial, finding the public url

Darl Converse Logic App example

This tutorial will show you how to use Darl Converse to create an email conversation with a client.

Creating a Logic App

For this example, we need three elements, two of which are Office365 connectors and the other is our DarlConverse API app.

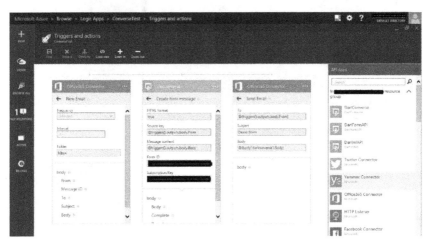

Figure 47, Tutorial, A full logic app.

Add the elements in the order Office365, Darl Converse, Office365, setting the first to trigger on a new email, the second to use the onllty method, **Create Form Message** and the last to Send Email. Each of the inputs can be set as shown.

Note that the messages are set to HTML in Darl Converse. The Send Email Office365 needs to be set to send a response in HTML too.

The Office365 elements will need to be authorized. For our example we set up an account called forms@docandys.com just for this example. The example rule set chosen calculates the UK tax take for a particular income.

An example run

Sending an email to the selected account triggers the Logic App, which then calls Darl Converse with the body. Our initial email contained only a general signature.

Darl Converse starts a new session with the source email address as the key, and creates a question set body to send as a response to the message.

UK Tax and NI calculator

Answer the following:

What is your wage per year? [0.00 -> 2000000.00]   _____

Any dividend income? (Give the value after corporation taxes) [0.00 -> 1000000.00]   _____

Your age in years [0.00 -> 120.00]   _____

Are you registered as blind? [True / False]   _____

Are you married? (Only matters over age 75) [True / False]   _____

Figure 48, Tutorial, the first email

Respond to the email by editing the text on the dotted lines.

From: forms
Sent: 09 August 2015 13:20
To: ▉▉▉▉▉▉▉▉▉▉▉▉▉▉▉▉▉▉▉▉▉▉▉▉▉▉▉▉▉
Subject: Demo Form

UK Tax and NI calculator

Answer the following:

What is your wage per year? [0.00 -> 2000000.00]   __50000____

Any dividend income? (Give the value after corporation taxes) [0.00 -> 1000000.00]   __45000___

Your age in years [0.00 -> 120.00]   __33___

Are you registered as blind? [True / False]   __False___

Are you married? (Only matters over age 75) [True / False]   __True____

Figure 49, Tutorial, responding to the email

Sending the email back will trigger the Logic App again. This time a cached session exists with the sending email as the key.

Darl Converse reads the email contents, looking for ids embedded in the original html and reads the values.

The response email is generated by the Darl Forms back end and converted to email compatible HTML.

Calculated results

Total taxes, per year 21133.80
Total taxes, per month 1761.15
National Insurance, per year 4337.32
National Insurance, per month 361.44
Your take home pay, per month 6516.96
Employers' NI, per year 5866.66
Percentage of the cost of your employment paid in tax 25.50

Figure 50, tutorial, the returned response.

Possible additions to the Logic App

This example has the usagemapId, identifying the rule set project to run, hard wired. One might easily get this from the subject of the incoming email. It is only required at the start of the session and cached thereafter. Some extra programming using the CsScripting API app could add the ability to send simple friendly names in the subject and map these to the project ids, which are nor particularly friendly.

All the data generated by this conversation can be used for for further processing. Another App could be arranged to be dependent on Darl Converse, taking either the Report, which contains formatted results, or the list of name-value pairs in the Values. Rather than calling this every time data is exchanged, you could add the condition that the Darl

Converse output **Complete** be true, which occurs only at the end of the conversation when all data and results/inferences have been generated.

Using the app with the Twitter connector, Twilio, etc.

This App also functions with text based media like twitter. Since multiple questions are unlikely to fit into the character limits, these are best set to be run one question at a time. To achieve this set the number of questions to 1 in the Form editor. Set the Darl Converse HTML Format input to *False*. In this case Darl Converse will look for a single item in the response tweet, text or whatever and attempt to convert it to the required format. If the conversion fails, the same question will be resent.

Using the Forms API directly

You can call the underlying DARL API directly for functionality outside of Logic Apps or Azure.

The general process

For a forms display of some kind there are three calls you need :

QSet_Get which opens the initial form conversation, QSet_Post which exchanges data with the conversation and QSet_Delete which acts as a "back" button.

The QSet_Get call is used initially. You call it with your subscription key and the id of the project you are using. It returns a QuestionSetProxy class. This contains an id in ieToken which represents the current conversation. Use this, rather than the project key in all further transactions.

The QuestionSetProxy also contains the first questions. The number of these is the number of unanswered, necessary questions or the form editor default question count, whichever is smaller. The questions are formatted as QuestionProxy classes.

You should display these questions and insert the responses back into your copy of the initial QuestionSetProxy. You then continue the process by calling QSet_Post with the updated QuestionSetProxy, which returns a new version of the same. This process continues until the QuestionSetProxy.Complete flag becomes true. At that point the list of questions will be empty and some responses will be available in the responses list. You should display these to the user. At any time if the QuestionSetProxy.CanUnwind flag is true you can call QSet_Delete function to delete the last set of answers. This will return a new QuestionSetProxy reflecting the previous state of the system.

Displaying questions

How you display the questions is very much up to you. Different media will have different requirements. DarlConverse, for instance is an API app that will communicate with emails and social media. For emails formatting must be entirely textual. For a web or App based interface you can use controls. Questions can be of three types, and each can be displayed differently.

numeric	displayable as edit controls with range validation, spinners or sliders
categorical	displayable as a drop down control filled from the categories property
textual	displayable as an edit or text control with optional regular expression validation

Inserting the responses

Each QuestionProxy has an SResponse and a DResponse property. For numeric inputs put a double value into DResponse, for categorical or textual put a text response into SResponse. For categorical questions the response should match exactly one of the categories.

Displaying responses

Again this is down to you how these are displayed. We support a variety of representations. Numeric values can be displayed textually or as a Score Bar. For the latter we supply the numeric range of the score bar, the actual value to display and text to put to the left and right of the bar. Textual values are either just text or a link to take the user off to some other page.

Reporting

In many usage scenarios you will want to do something else with the data collected other than display it to the user. You can individually decide which outputs of the rule set to display to the user as responses. The entire data set, including questions and all the inferred output values will be available QuestionSetProxy.values property as a set of name value pairs. It is therefore straightforward to trigger some other process and pass this data set on.

External references

Dr Andy's IP main site	http://www.docandys.com
Dr Andy's Developer Portal	https://darlinf.portal.azure-api.net
Dr Andy's documentation	http://docs.docandys.com/en/latest/DarlDocs/Darl/
DarlCommon on NuGet	http://www.nuget.org/packages/DarlCommon/
GitHub API app and docs repository	https://github.com/drandysip

Appendix

DARL language definition

The DARL language is intended to permit both software tools and humans to record and re-use knowledge in the form of "if..then" rules.

The language is simple and intuitive. Given the appropriate tooling, non-programmers should be able to use it.

Primitive elements

The following primitive elements are defined in DARL.

Identifiers

Identifiers are names used to identify inputs, outputs, constants, strings, rulesets, mapinputs and mapoutputs.

They follow the convention of C#, namely:

- They cannot start with a number

- They cannot contain spaces

- They are case sensitive

- They can only contain letters, numbers and the "_" character.

Numeric literals

These follow C#, so they can be integers or floating point numbers with optional exponent.

String literals

These are pieces of text delineated with the " or ' characters.

Terminators

These are characters that delineate different sections of DARL. they are:

; - marking the end of a rule or definition

{ } - marking the beginning and end of a block - used in set and ruleset definitions

( ) - marking the beginning and end of a list in functions

, - separating elements of a list

Keywords
These are pieces of text that have specific meaning in the DARL language. they are:

"{", "}", "(", ")", ",", ";", ".", "if", "then", "will", "be", "confidence", "input", "output", "numeric",
"categorical","arity","presence","string","constant", "or",
"and","not","is","*","/","-
","+","%","^",">","<",">=","<=","anything","textual",
"maximum","minimum","sum","product","fuzzytuple","sigmoid","normprob","round","ruleset","wire"," mapinput","mapoutput","pattern"

Keywords are always lower case.

Composite identifiers
When connecting to inputs or outputs of a ruleset it is necessary to use the name of the ruleset and the input or output name.

This is achieved by concatenating the ruleset name and the i/o name with a "." separator.

```
rulesetname.inputname
```

Comments
Comments are freely permitted in code. They follow the C#/Java form:

```
//single line comment
```

```
/*bounded   comment */
```

Top level elements
These elements are concerned with inputs and outputs at the highest level, and the definition of rulesets.

Mapinputs

These define the inputs at the top or "map" level.

These will accept external values during the machine learning or inference process.

They take two parameters, the first, which is mandatory, is an identifier naming the mapinput, the second optional parameter is a string containing navigation text for machine learning.

```
mapinput fred "/fred/text()"
```

Mapoutputs

These define the outputs at the top or "map" level.

These will generate values during the machine learning or inference process.

They take two parameters, the first, which is mandatory, is an identifier naming the mapoutput, the second optional parameter is a string containing navigation text for machine learning.

```
mapoutput bill "/bill/text()"
```

Wires

These connect up the various elements at the top level.

They take two parameters, the first is an identifier naming the source, the second parameter is an identifier naming the destination. Both may be composite identifiers

Sources can be mapinputs or ruleset outputs. Destinations may be mapoutputs or ruleset inputs.

```
wire input1 ruleset1.input1
```

```
wire ruleset2.output1 ruleset3.input2
```

The DARL parser checks for impossible combinations, such as connecting two ruleset outputs.

The Visual Studio DARL designer makes these checks dynamically.

A further constraint is that connections between rulesets are only possible where the data types match.

Rulesets

These define the block of code corresponding to a ruleset.

A ruleset is a unit of processing, with an analogy to the class in conventional programming.

They take two parameters, the first, which is mandatory, is an identifier naming the ruleset, the second optional parameter is a keyword identifying if the ruleset will be subject to machine learning.

Choices here are

- manual - The ruleset contents will be created by hand

- supervised - The ruleset will be created by supervised machine learning

- unsupervised - The ruleset will be created by unsupervised learning

- reinforcement - The ruleset will be created by reinforcement learning

```
ruleset ruleset1 supervised { ruleset content }
```

The pattern

When the contents of one or more rule sets are to be set by machine learning, then a data source must be connected to the DARL file.

Machine learning is based on learning associations between or within inputs and/or outputs. Generally these data values are presented as a series of patterns.

The optional pattern element permits you to define how to find those patterns in the language appropriate to the data source. This might be XPath for an XML source, or SQL for a database.

There should only be one pattern element in a DARL source file.

Patterns take one parameter, the string containing the navigation text to identify the pattern.

```
pattern "//pattern"
```

Ruleset level elements

These elements are concerned with inputs and outputs within a ruleset and the contents of the rules.

inputs

These define the inputs at the ruleset level.

These will accept external values during the machine learning or inference process.

They take several parameters, the first, which is mandatory, is the data type of the input, the second also mandatory parameter is an identifier naming the input.

Choices here are

- numeric - the input value will be a number.

- categorical - the input value will be text falling into one of a set of categories.

- textual - the input value will be a string.

```
input numeric fred;
```

Numeric inputs can optionally contain a series of fuzzy set definitions, while categorical inputs can have a series of categories.

Fuzzy sets require an identifier to name the set and between 1 and 4 numeric literals, in ascending order, to define the set.

```
input numeric fred {{small, 1, 2, 3},{medium, 2, 3,
4},{large, 3, 4, 5}};
```

Inputs can have any number of fuzzy sets, though each set name must be unique. Ideally the ruleset writer will choose meaningful names and ensure that the set ranges match the names.

So, as above, the medium set ought to be greater than the small set. This is an element of style that the DARL parser cannot enforce.

If machine learning of a ruleset is employed, fuzzy sets will be generated automatically from the data.

Category definitions

Categorical variables are very common. They are multi-choice variables, like male/female or single/married/separated/divorced.

A category definition is a sequence of categories, that can be either identifiers or string literals.

```
input categorical fred {true,false};
```

If machine learning of a ruleset is employed, categories will be generated automatically from the data.

Outputs

These define the outputs at the ruleset level.

These will generate values during the machine learning or inference process.

They take several parameters, the first, which is mandatory, is the data type of the output, the second also mandatory parameter is is an identifier naming the input.

Choices here are

- numeric - the input value will be a number.

- categorical - the input value will be text falling into one of a set of categories.

```
output numeric fred;
```

Numeric inputs can optionally contain a series of fuzzy set definitions, while categorical inputs can have a series of categories.

Fuzzy set definitions

Fuzzy sets require an identifier to name the set and between 1 and 4 numeric literals, in ascending order, to define the set.

```
output numeric fred {{small, 1, 2, 3},{medium, 2, 3,
4},{large, 3, 4, 5}};
```

Outputs can have any number of fuzzy sets, though each set name must be unique. Ideally the ruleset writer will choose meaningful names and ensure that the set ranges match the names.

So, as above, the medium set ought to be greater than the small set. This is an element of style that the DARL parser cannot enforce.

If machine learning of a ruleset is employed, fuzzy sets will be generated automatically from the data.

Category definitions

Categorical variables are very common. They are multi-choice variables, like male/female or single/married/separated/divorced.

A category definition is a sequence of categories, that can be either identifiers or string literals.

```
output categorical fred {true,false};
```

If machine learning of a ruleset is employed, categories will be generated automatically from the data.

Constants

This permits the definition of numeric constants.

90

Since constants are frequently re-used and it is better practice to keep them in one place, DARL does not allow the use of numeric literals inside rules. Instead you should define a numeric constant and use the name of that constant.

A constant has two parameters, the identifier naming the constant and a numeric literal.

```
constant Age_related_income_limit 24000;
```

String Constants
This permits the definition of string constants.

Since constants are frequently re-used and it is better practice to keep them in one place, DARL does not allow the use of string literals inside rules. Instead you should define a string constant and use the name of that constant.

A string constant has two parameters, the identifier naming the constant and a string literal.

```
string regex1 "*A|B";
```

Sequence Constants
This permits the definition of sequence constants.

Since constants are frequently re-used and it is better practice to keep them in one place, DARL does not allow the use of sequence literals inside rules. Instead you should define a sequence constant and use the name of that constant.

A sequence constant has two parameters, the identifier naming the constant and a sequence literal. The latter defines a sequence of string literals and/or lists of string literals.

```
string seq1 {"fred",{"jane","samantha"},"bill"};
```

The above is interpreted as a sequence of literals as, "fred", followed by "jane" or "samantha", followed by "bill".

Sequences are an extension to DARL used in DAPL.

Rule level elements

Part of the flexibility of DARL is the ability to represent many kinds of relationships with one structure

The fundamental structure of a rule is as follows:

```
if < conditional expression > then < output identifier
> will be < RHS expression > < optional confidence
value >;
```

Since outputs can be numeric or categorical, the RHS expression syntax depends on the type of the output. Choices are:

- Categorical output: The RHS can only be a category defined in the list of categories for that output

- Numerical output: The RHS can be a fuzzy set defined in the list of sets for that output

- Numerical output: The RHS can be a numeric expression that is evaluated dynamically.

Conditional Expressions

This is a fuzzy or Boolean logic expression. The degree of truth associated with it as it is evaluated is used to determine the rules precedence against other rules containing the same output identifier.

There are several logical operators that may be used at the top level:

- anything: If used this must be the only operator in the top-level conditional expression and always evaluates to truth 1.0.

  ```
  if anything then a will be b;
  ```

- and: gives the fuzzy logic "and" of the operands either side, implemented as the minimum of their degrees of truth.

  ```
  if a is b and c is d then f will be q;
  ```

- or: gives the fuzzy logic "or" of the operands either side, implemented as the maximum of their degrees of truth.

```
if a is b or c is d then f will be q;
```

- not: gives the fuzzy logic "not" of the single operand following, implemented as 1 - its degrees of truth.

```
if not a is b then f will be q;
```

- is: evaluates the input's or output's fuzzy value on the left hand side against the expression on the right hand side.

```
if a is b then f will be q;
```

Since the input or output could be numeric, categorical or textual (inputs only) there are several possible combinations.

The input or output is categorical, the RHS can only be a category defined for that input or output.

```
if a is false then b will be true;
```

The input or output is numeric, the RHS can be a set defined for that input or output.

```
if a is large then b will be true;
```

The input or output is numeric, the RHS can be a comparison operation followed by a numeric expression.

```
if a is < c + d then b will be true;
```

Comparison operators can be >, <, <=, >=, =, !=, interpreted as greater than, less than, greater than or equal to, less than or equal to, equal to and not equal to respectively.

The input is textual, the RHS can only be a textual comparison operation.

```
if a is match(string) then b will be true;
```

Numeric Expressions

This is an algebraic expression, following the rules of Fuzzy Arithmetic, see Introduction to Fuzzy Arithmetic

The operands can only be numeric inputs or outputs, numeric constants, built in functions or other numeric operators.

The operators available are:

+: Addition.

```
if a is = b + c then d will be true;
```

-: Subtraction.

```
if a is = b - c then d will be true;
```

*: Multiplication.

```
if a is = b * c then d will be true;
```

/: Division.

```
if a is = b / c then d will be true;
```

^: Power.

```
if a is = b ^ c then d will be true;
```

%: Modulo.

```
if a is = b % c then d will be true;
```

For built in functions, the parameters are separated by commas and can each be numeric expressions.

Built in functions are:

sum: The sum of a set of values.

```
if a is = sum(b,c,d) then p will be q;
```

product: The product of a set of values.

```
if a is = product(b,c,d) then p will be q;
```

maximum: The greatest of a set of values.

```
if a is = maximum(b,c,d) then p will be q;
```

minimum: The smallest of a set of values.

```
if a is = minimum(b,c,d) then p will be q;
```

normprob: The Gaussian probability of a normalized value (average = 0, SD = 1).

```
if a is = normprob(b) then p will be q;
```

Note a single operand.

round: the first operand is rounded to the accuracy set by the 2nd. Non-fuzzy

```
if a is = round(b,c) then p will be q;
```

Note only two operands.

Optional Confidence Value

Rules can have an optional confidence value, in the range 0.0 to 1.0.

If no confidence is specified, the default confidence is 1.0.

The confidence value corresponds to the maximum degree of truth associated with that rule.

For rule sets created via machine learning, this is associated with the support the data gives to this rule.

For rules created by hand, you can create default behavior, i.e. you can specify a rule that fires if others don't, by defining a rule with low confidence.

```
if anything then b will be false confidence 0.5;
```

Darl REST API structures

The following structures are used to pass data to and from the REST API.

Class DarlVar

A general representation of a data value containing related uncertainty information from a fuzzy/possibilistic perspective.

Properties

approximate

boolean

Indicates approximation has taken place in calculating the values. Under some circumstances the coordinates of the fuzzy number in "values" may not exactly represent the "cuts" values.

categories

Dictionary<string, double>

list of categories, each indexed against a truth value.

dataType

Enum DataType

Gets or sets the type of the data.

name

string

Gets or sets the name.

sequence

List<List<string>>

Gets or sets the sequence.

unknown

boolean

This result is unknown if true.

Value

string

Single central or most confident value, expressed as a string or double.

values

List<double>

The array containing the up to 4 values representing the fuzzy number.

Since all fuzzy numbers used by DARL are convex, i,e. their envelope doesn't have any in-folding sections, the user can specify numbers with a simple sequence of doubles. So 1 double represents a crisp or singleton value. 2 doubles represent an interval, 3 a triangular fuzzy set, 4 a trapezoidal fuzzy set. The values must be ordered in ascending value, but it is permissible for two or more to hold the same value.

weight

double

The confidence placed in this result

Enumerations

DataType

The type of data stored in the DarlVar

values	use	integer value
numeric	Numeric including fuzzy	0

values	use	integer value
categorical	One or more categories with confidences	1
textual	a text string	2
sequence	a text sequence	3

Example Json

```
{
    "name": "string",
    "unknown": true,
    "weight": 0,
    "values": [
        0
    ],
    "categories": {},
    "approximate": true,
    "dataType": 0,
    "sequence": [
        [
            "string"
        ]
    ],
    "Value": "string"
}
```

Class DaslState

A time stamped state of a system, reconstructible from the associated values.

Properties

timeStamp

DateTime

Gets or sets the time stamp for this state.

values

List<DarlVar>

Gets or sets the values.

Class FormFormat

Contains formatting information for a Darl Form

Properties

DefaultQuestions

integer

Gets or sets the default number of questions.

InputFormatList

List<InputFormat>

A list of one or more input definitions

OutputFormatList

List<OutputFormat>

A list of one or more output definitions

Class InputFormat
The format of a Darl input

Properties

Categories

List<string>

Gets or sets the categories.

Increment

double

Gets or sets the increment used when editing values with a spinner type control.

InType

InputType

Gets or sets the type of the input.

MaxLength

integer

Gets or sets the maximum length of a textual input

Name

string

Gets or sets the name of the input.

NumericMax

double

Gets or sets the numeric maximum expected value for use in validation and slider controls.

NumericMin

double

Gets or sets the numeric minimum expected value for use in validation and slider controls.

Regex

string

Gets or sets a regular expression used to validate textual inputs.

ShowSets

boolean

Gets or sets a value indicating whether to show set names as if they were categories.

Enumerations
InputType

The data type of the input

values	use	integer value
categorical	categorical input	1
numeric	Numerical input	0
textual	Textual input	2

Class LanguageFormat
Language format

Properties

DefaultLanguage

string

The default language as a two character ISO name.

LanguageList

List<LanguageText>

Gets or sets the language list.

Class LanguageText
An individual text item

Properties

Name

string

The system name for this text derived from the associated Darl input or output, or one of the predefined types.

Text

string

The text to display for the default language.

VariantList

List<VariantText>

A list of language versions of the text.

Class OutputFormat
Defines the format of a Darl output

Properties

Hide

boolean

If true this output is not displayed to the user.

Name

string

The name of the output matching that in the associated Darl file.

OutputType

OutType

Gets or sets the type of the output.

ScoreBarColor

string

Gets or sets the color of the score bar if used.

ScoreBarMaxVal

double

Gets or sets the score bar maximum value if used.

ScoreBarMinVal

double

Gets or sets the score bar minimum value if used.

Uncertainty

boolean

Gets or sets a value indicating whether uncertainty information is displayed.

displayType

DisplayType

Determines how the output is displayed.

ValueFormat

string

Gets or sets the value format. This is a string determining how numerical values are displayed.

Enumerations

DisplayType

The possible display types

values	use	integer value
Link	Display as a link	3
ScoreBar	display as a bar	2
Text	Display as text	1

OutType

The possible output types

values	use	integer value
categorical	a categorical output	1

values	use	integer value
numeric	a numeric output	0

Class QuestionProxy

Represents a single question displayed on a form

Properties

categories

List<string>

A list of permissible categories if categorical. Use as choices in a drop down.

DResponse

double

A numeric response from the user.

Format

string

A regular expression that can be used to validate a textual input.

Increment

double

The increment to use for number selection - 1 for integers, 0 for continuum etc.

Maxval

double

If numeric the upper bound (+infinity if unbounded)

Minval

double

If numeric the lower bound (-infinity if unbounded)

path

string

Gets or sets the path. (reserved for future use)

qtype

QType

The type of the question

Reference

string

The id of the question

Sresponse

string

textual response from the user.

Text

string

The text of the question

Enumerations

QType

Used to define the data type

values	use	integer value
categorical	categorical input	1
numeric	Numerical input	0
textual	Textual input	2

Class QuestionSetProxy
The set of questions or responses and status info.

Properties

CanUnwind

boolean

Indicates that the user can unwind a previous set of answers

Complete

boolean

True if questionnaire is completely satisfied.

ieToken

GUID represented as string

Identifies this questionnaire run

Language

string

2 character iso of the language requested

PercentComplete

double

Percentage complete, 0-100

Preamble

string

text displayed before form

QuestionHeader

string

111

text displayed before questions

questions

List<QuestionProxy>

Zero or more questions

ResponseHeader

string

text displayed before results

responses

List<ResponseProxy>

Zero or more responses

values

Dictionary<string, string>

The values for reporting, valid if Complete is true.

Example Json

```
{
  "questions": [
    {
      "Reference": "string",
      "Text": "string",
      "path": "string",
      "format": "string",
      "qtype": 0,
      "minval": 0,
      "maxval": 0,
      "increment": 0,
      "categories": [
        "string"
      ],
      "SResponse": "string",
      "DResponse": 0
```

```json
        }
    ],
    "responses": [
        {
            "rtype": 0,
            "Preamble": "string",
            "MainText": "string",
            "Annotation": "string",
            "Value": 0,
            "LowText": "string",
            "HighText": "string",
            "Color": "string",
            "MinVal": 0,
            "MaxVal": 0,
            "format": "string"
        }
    ],
    "PercentComplete": 0,
    "Complete": true,
    "ieToken": "string",
    "ResponseHeader": "string",
    "QuestionHeader": "string",
    "Preamble": "string",
    "CanUnwind": true,
    "Language": "string",
    "values": {}
}
```

Class ResponseProxy

Represents an inferred response from the inference engine being displayed to the user.

Properties

Annotation

string

The description of the answer

Color

string

The color of the filled section of the score bar

format

string

The format for numeric answers.

HighText

string

the text to the right of the score bar if used

LowText

string

The text to the left of the score bar if used

MainText

string

If text, the second bit of the text, the actual answer

MaxVal

double

the value representing 100% on the score bar or the upper possibility bound

MinVal

double

The value representing 0 on the score bar or the lower possibility bound

Preamble

string

Preamble text. This is used if a responseProxy is not associated with an output, but contains a message.

rtype

RType

the type of response

Value

double

A numeric answer value if a Score Bar is used.

Enumerations
RType

The types of response possible

values	use	integer value
Link	Display as a link	3
ScoreBar	display as a bar	2

values	use	integer value
Text	Display as text	1
Preamble	Display the preamble text only	0

Class VariantText

Holds a language version of a particular piece of text used in a form.

Properties

Language

string

The language as a two character ISO name.

Text

string

The text in the given language

Darl REST API calls

The following are the calls you can use with your own code to access the Darl API.

Some of these calls are for future expansion, and other calls will be added in the near future.

DaplInfo_Get

This call relates to the Darl Policy extension to Darl.

This call retrieves information for a particular pedigree index.

Request parameters

pedigree	string	The pedigree
subscription-key	string	The client's key

Responses

OK 200

Json

```
{
   "description": "string",
   "type": 0
}
```

DaplMap_Post

This call relates to the Darl Policy extension to Darl.

Gets a prototype map from a set of data values supplied in Json or XML in the request body.

The prototype map contains a description of the enclosed data types using the DAPL model.

Request parameters

name	string	The name of the object type
subscription-key	string	The client's key
path	string	The path returning these objects from a selected data set, in JPath/XPath or whatever

Request body

Any Json/XML object

Responses

OK 200

Json

```
{
  "attributes": [
    {
      "name": "string",
      "path": "string",
      "pedigree": [
        [
          "string"
        ]
      ]
    }
  ],
  "name": "string",
  "path": "string",
```

```
    "pedigree": [
      [
        "string"
      ]
    ]
}
```

DarlInf_Get

Gets a list of inputs with specimen values.

Request parameters

id	string	The usage map identifier
subscription-key	string	The client's key

Responses

OK 200

Returns an array of DarlVar objects.

Json

```
[
  {
    "name": "string",
    "unknown": true,
    "weight": 0,
    "values": [
      0
    ],
    "categories": {},
    "approximate": true,
    "dataType": 0,
    "sequence": [
      [
        "string"
      ]
    ],
    "Value": "string"
  }
]
```

DarlInf_Post
Evaluates a set of data against a DARL source.

Request parameters

id	string	The usage map identifier
subscription-key	string	The client's key

Request body

An array of DarlVar objects – possibly derived from DarInf_Get.

Responses

OK 200

Returns an array of DarlVar objects.

Json

```
[
  {
    "name": "string",
    "unknown": true,
    "weight": 0,
    "values": [
      0
    ],
    "categories": {},
    "approximate": true,
    "dataType": 0,
    "sequence": [
      [
        "string"
      ]
    ],
    "Value": "string"
  }
]
```

DarlSimp_Get

Gets a list of inputs with specimen values for the simplified interface.

Request parameters

id	string	The usage map identifier
subscription-key	string	The client's key

Responses

OK 200

Returns an array of name-value pairs.

DarlSimp_Post

Evaluates a set of data against a DARL source using the simplified interface.

Request parameters

id	string	The usage map identifier
subscription-key	string	The client's key

Request body

An array of name value pairs possible derived from DarlSimp_Get.

Responses

OK 200

Returns an array of name-value pairs for the inputs and inferred outputs.

DaslInf_Post

Runs a simulation using the supplied sequence of states. If attribute values are empty they are filled in in the copy of the sequence returned.

id	string	The usage map identifier
subscription-key	string	The client's key

Request body

An array of DaslState objects representing the history.

Responses

OK 200

Returns an array of DaslState objects.

Json

```
[
 {
   "timeStamp": "2015-12-03T12:34:00.844Z"
   "values": [
    {
     "name": "string",
     "unknown": true,
     "weight": 0,
     "values": [
      0
     ],
     "categories": {},
     "approximate": true,
     "dataType": 0,
     "sequence": [
      [
       "string"
      ]
```

```
        ],
        "Value": "string"
      }
    ]
  }
]
```

QSet_Delete

Deletes the last set of responses, acting as a "back" function.

Request parameters

id	string	The usage map identifier
subscription-key	string	The client's key

Responses

OK 200

Returns a QuestionSetProxy object containing the previous state.

QSet_Get

Gets the first set of questions for a new questionnaire session.

Request parameters

id	string	The usage map identifier
subscription-key	string	The client's key

Responses

OK 200

Returns a QuestionSetProxy object containing the questions

QSet_Post

Sends the responses and gets a new set of questions or results.

Request parameters

id	string	The usage map identifier
subscription-key	string	The client's key

Request Body

The previously returned QuestionSetProxy object populated with results.

Responses

OK 200

Returns a QuestionSetProxy object containing the questions

QSet_Put
Sends the responses.

Request parameters

id	string	The usage map identifier
subscription-key	string	The client's key

Request Body

The previously returned QuestionSetProxy object populated with results.

Note – To get the next set of objects, if using PUT,GET, rather than just POST, issue a GET with the id set to the ieToken value of the last QuestionSetProxy.

Responses

OK 200

Index

www.ingramcontent.com/pod-product-compliance
Lightning Source LLC
Chambersburg PA
CBHW071220050326
40689CB00011B/2385